Sansevieria

SNOW
IS
FALLING

# SNOW

by FRANKLYN M. BRANLEY

illustrated by HELEN STONE

THOMAS Y. CROWELL COMPANY · NEW YORK

IS

FALLING

# LET'S-READ-AND-FIND-OUT BOOKS

Special Adviser: *DR. ROMA GANS*, Professor Emeritus of Childhood Education, Teachers College, Columbia University.
Editor: *DR. FRANKLYN M. BRANLEY*, Coordinator of Educational Services, American Museum—Hayden Planetarium, consultant on science in elementary education.

*A Tree Is a Plant*

*How a Seed Grows*

*Seeds by Wind and Water*

*Down Come the Leaves*

*The Wonder of Stones*

*Big Tracks, Little Tracks*

*Animals in Winter*

*Starfish*

*Sandpipers*

*Birds Eat and Eat and Eat*

*Fireflies in the Night*

*Where the Brook Begins*

*The Clean Brook*

*Snow Is Falling*

*What Makes a Shadow?*

*Air Is All Around You*

*Rain and Hail*

*Upstairs and Downstairs*

*My Five Senses*

*Look at Your Eyes*

*My Hands*

*Find Out by Touching*

*Follow Your Nose*

*In the Night*

*The Listening Walk*

*How Many Teeth?*

*The Moon Seems to Change*

*What Makes Day and Night*

*The Sun: Our Nearest Star*

*The Big Dipper*

*Rockets and Satellites*

*What the Moon Is Like*

# SNOW
# IS
# FALLING

LET'S
READ
AND
FIND
OUT

Night has come and snow is falling.
It falls without a sound.

Look at the street light.
You can see snow falling in front of it.
The snow may fall all night.

The snow may fall all day.
The snow gets deeper and deeper.
Now the lawn is white.
The trees are white, and so are the roofs of houses.

Everything is covered.
Everything is quiet.
Everything is white.
Everything is cold.

It is always cold when snow falls.
It is so cold that water vapor
  freezes in the air.


This makes snowflakes.


Let a snowflake fall
  on your mitten.
The snowflake may be small.
It may be big.

If the snowflake is very small,
    look at it through a magnifying glass.
A magnifying glass makes things look bigger.

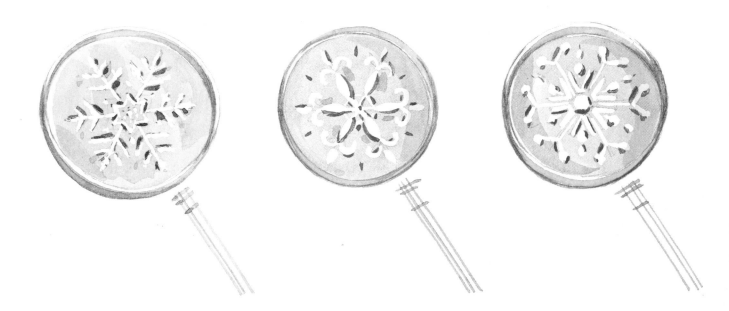

The snowflake will look like this,                or this,      or like this.
Count the sides on each snowflake. Each snowflake has six sides.
Each snowflake is different, but each one has six sides.

Sometimes snowflakes are wet and sticky.
When you walk in wet, sticky snow,
    you splash, and slip, and slide.

Sometimes snowflakes are light, dry, and fluffy.

Walking through light snow is fun.

You can kick it into the air.

You can scoop up a big shovelful of light, dry snow.

You can run and roll and ski in the snow.

You can slide on your sled.

You can build a snowman.

Snow can be fun, but what good is snow?
Is it good for plants? Is it good for animals?
Is it good for you and me?
Let's find out!

Snow covers plants that must stay in the ground all winter.
The snow is a blanket that covers the plants.
Because the plants are covered,
     the wind, ice, and cold cannot hurt them.

Plants that are covered with snow
can live through the cold winter.
Snow is good for plants.

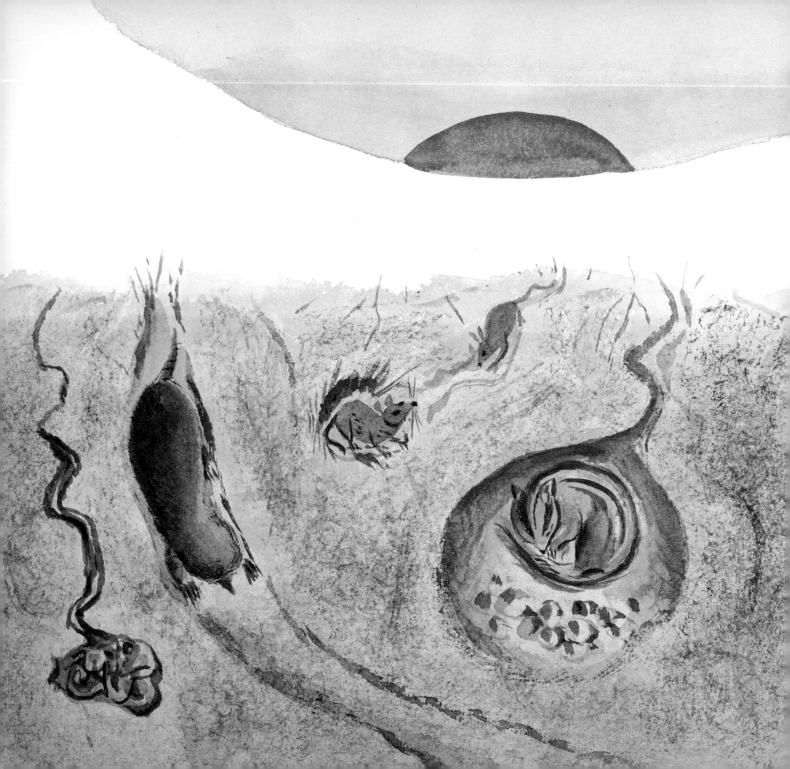

Snow is good for many animals, too.
Worms and mice, moles and chipmunks stay under the ground
  all winter.
The snow makes a blanket over the ground.
The blanket keeps the wind and cold from the animals.
Snow helps to keep them warm.
You can prove it.

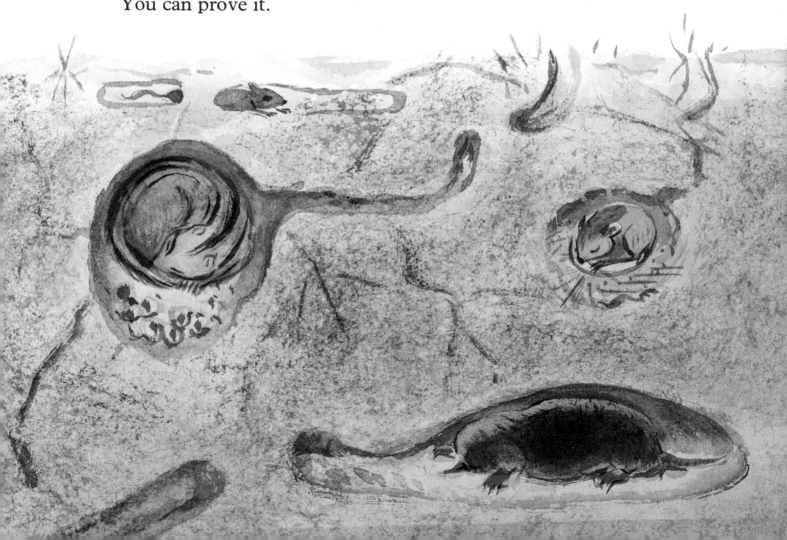

Get two thermometers like these.

Bury one thermometer in the snow.

Hang the other thermometer outdoors.

Hang it from a tree or alongside a window.
After an hour, uncover the thermometer
in the snow. What is the temperature?

Look at the other thermometer.
  What is the temperature?
Which is colder?
  Which is colder in the picture?
Snow protects many plants and animals
  from the wind and cold.

It protects people, too.

In the far north, Eskimos sometimes make houses of snow.

From the hard, packed snow they cut out blocks.

They pile the blocks high to make a snow house.

The snow house is called an igloo.
Inside the igloos, Eskimos keep snug and warm.

Snow is good in other ways.
Melted snow gives us water for our wells,
our streams, and our rivers.

When snow melts slowly, the water goes into the soil.
The soil becomes crumbly.
When winter is over, the sun warms the soil.
Plants grow well in the loose, moist, warm soil.

Food grows well in the loose, moist, warm soil.

Sometimes snow is not good.
When snow piles high, it may be
   so deep that animals cannot move.
The snow covers their food.

The deep snows of winter may melt fast in the spring.

There is more water than streams can carry.

The streams overflow.

Water spreads through towns and cities. There are floods.

When strong winds blow, the soft, quiet snow becomes
  a howling blizzard.
Deep drifts cover houses and barns, roads and cars.
A blizzard makes life hard for animals and people.

But snow can make life good.

Snow is fun to run, roll, and ski in.

Snow gives us water for wells, streams, and rivers.
Snow is good for farmers. Snow is good for plants.

It is good for you and me!

## ABOUT THE AUTHOR

Franklyn M. Branley is Associate Astronomer at the American Museum–Hayden Planetarium, where he has contact with audiences of all ages and where he directs the diverse educational program. For many years he has helped children learn scientific facts and principles at an early age without impairing their sense of wonder about the world they live in. Before coming to the Planetarium, Dr. Branley taught science at many grade levels, including the lower elementary grades, high school, college, and graduate school.

Dr. Branley received his training for teaching at the New York State College of Education at New Paltz, New York, at New York University, and Columbia University. He lives with his wife and two daughters in Woodcliff Lake, New Jersey.

## ABOUT THE ILLUSTRATOR

Helen Stone is a well-known illustrator of children's books. Because of her deep interest in conservation, she was especially pleased to provide the artwork for *Snow Is Falling*.

Mrs. Stone has studied at several art schools in London, Paris, and New York. She paints, writes poetry, and restores old houses. Mrs. Stone lives in East Hampton, New York, with her husband.